TIKI HUNT
INK YOUR WAY TO TIKI HEAVEN

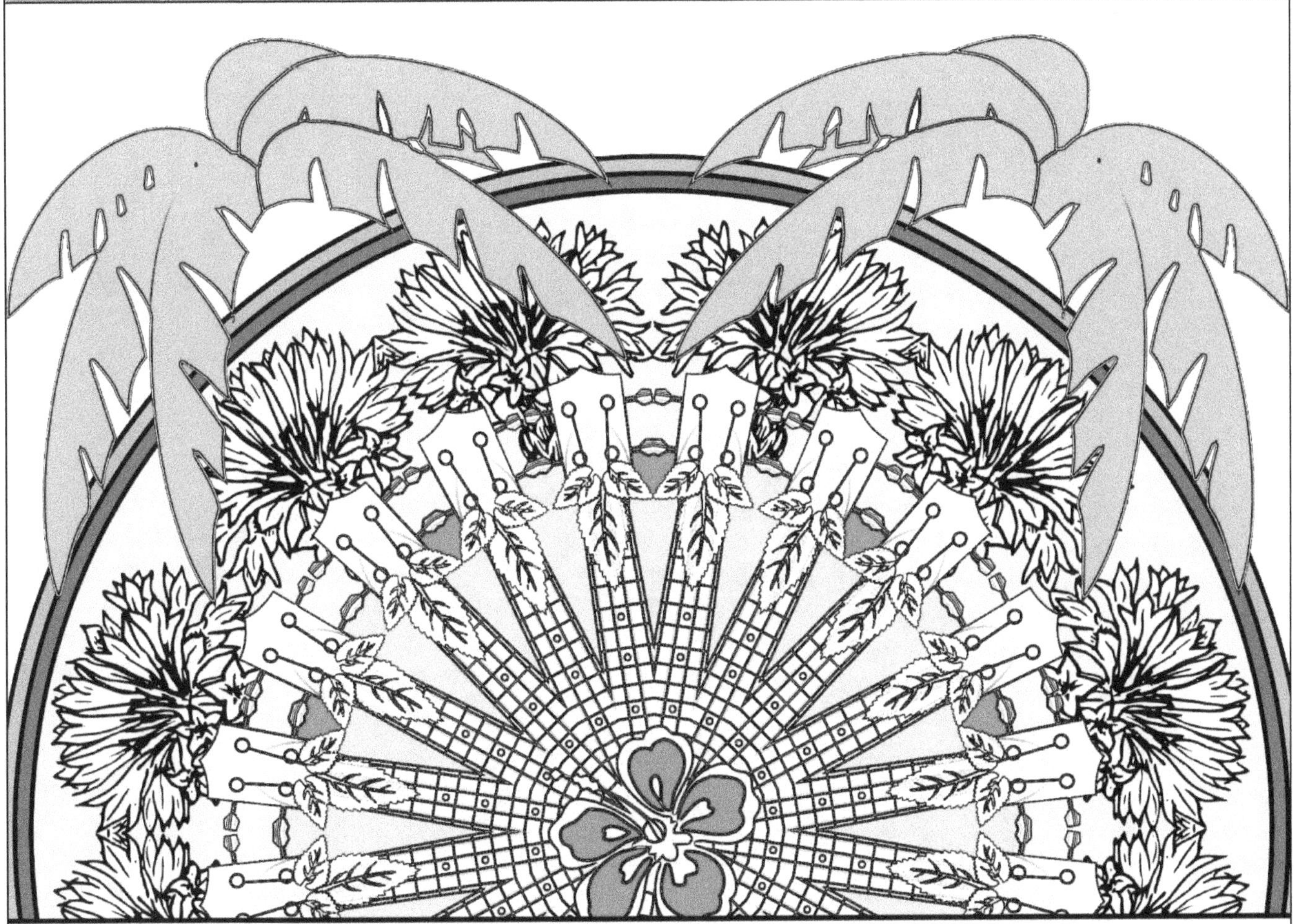

COLORING BOOKS FOR ADULTS

CLIPPEE COLORING BOOKS
BY JAKE WIDMER

Tiki Hunt: Ink Your Way to Tiki Heaven Coloring Books for Adults

Clippee Coloring

By Jake Widmer

PUBLISHED BY:
Jake Widmer
Copyright © 2015

_____

How to Use This Book

1) Open the book.

---

2) Turn off the TV.

---

3) Turn on your favorite relaxing music.

---

4) Pull out your favorite coloring pencils, crayons, or markers.

---

5) Dont answer that phone! In fact, put it away! ☺

---

6) Use your imagination and start coloring!

---

7) If you feel you've had enough, pick up where you left off at a later time...

---

8) If you haven't had enough... keep going!

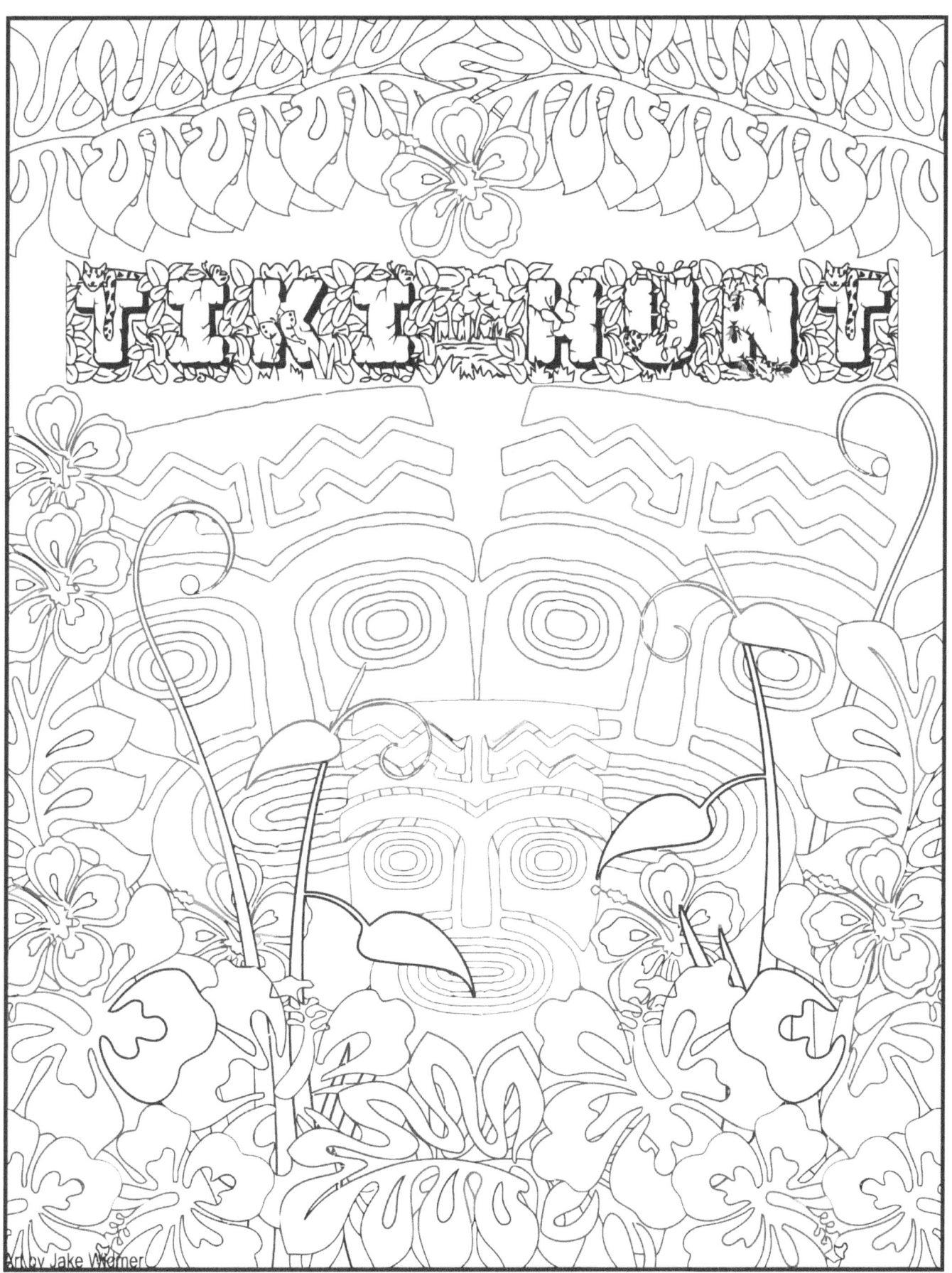

Art by Jake Werner

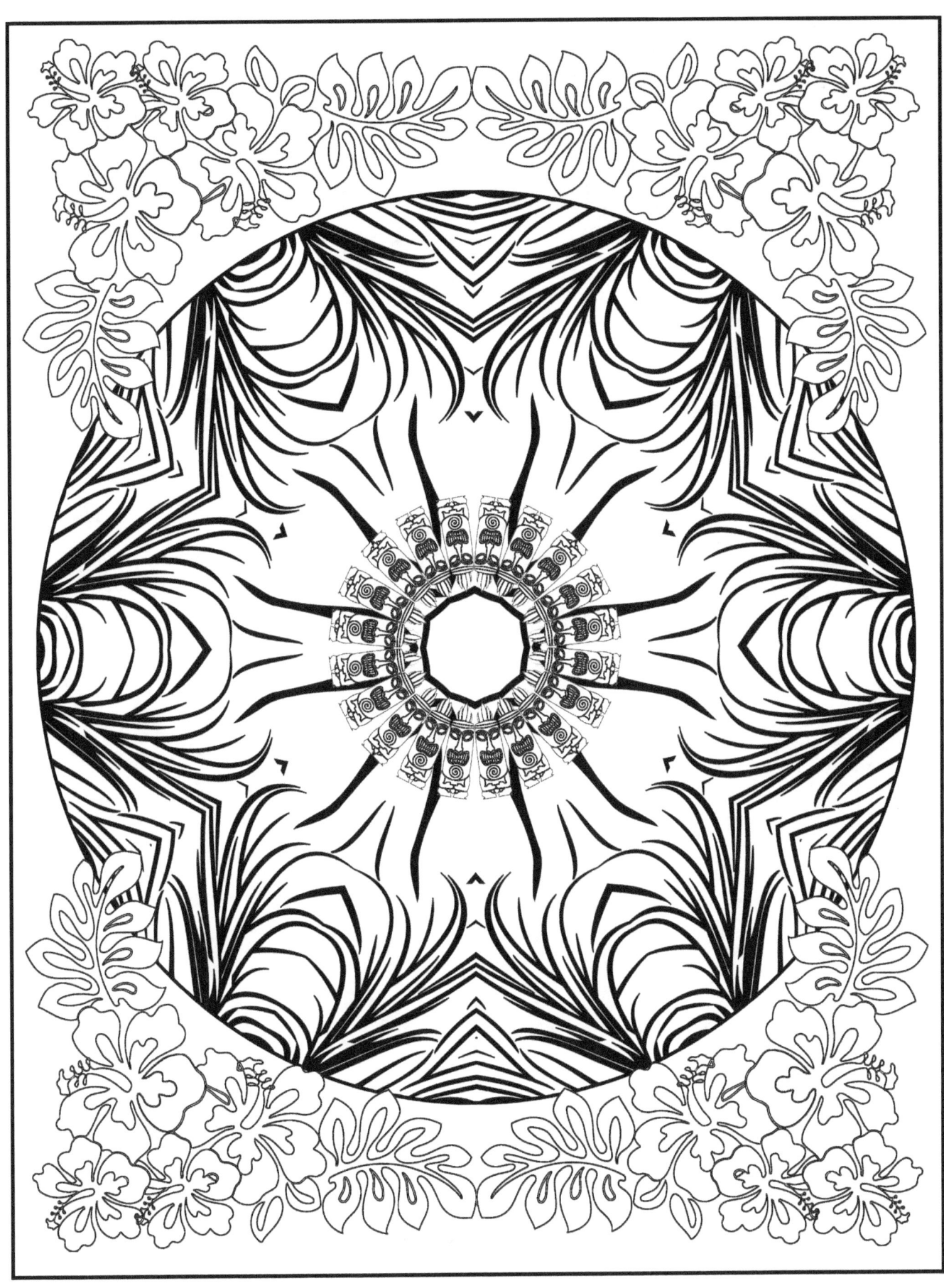

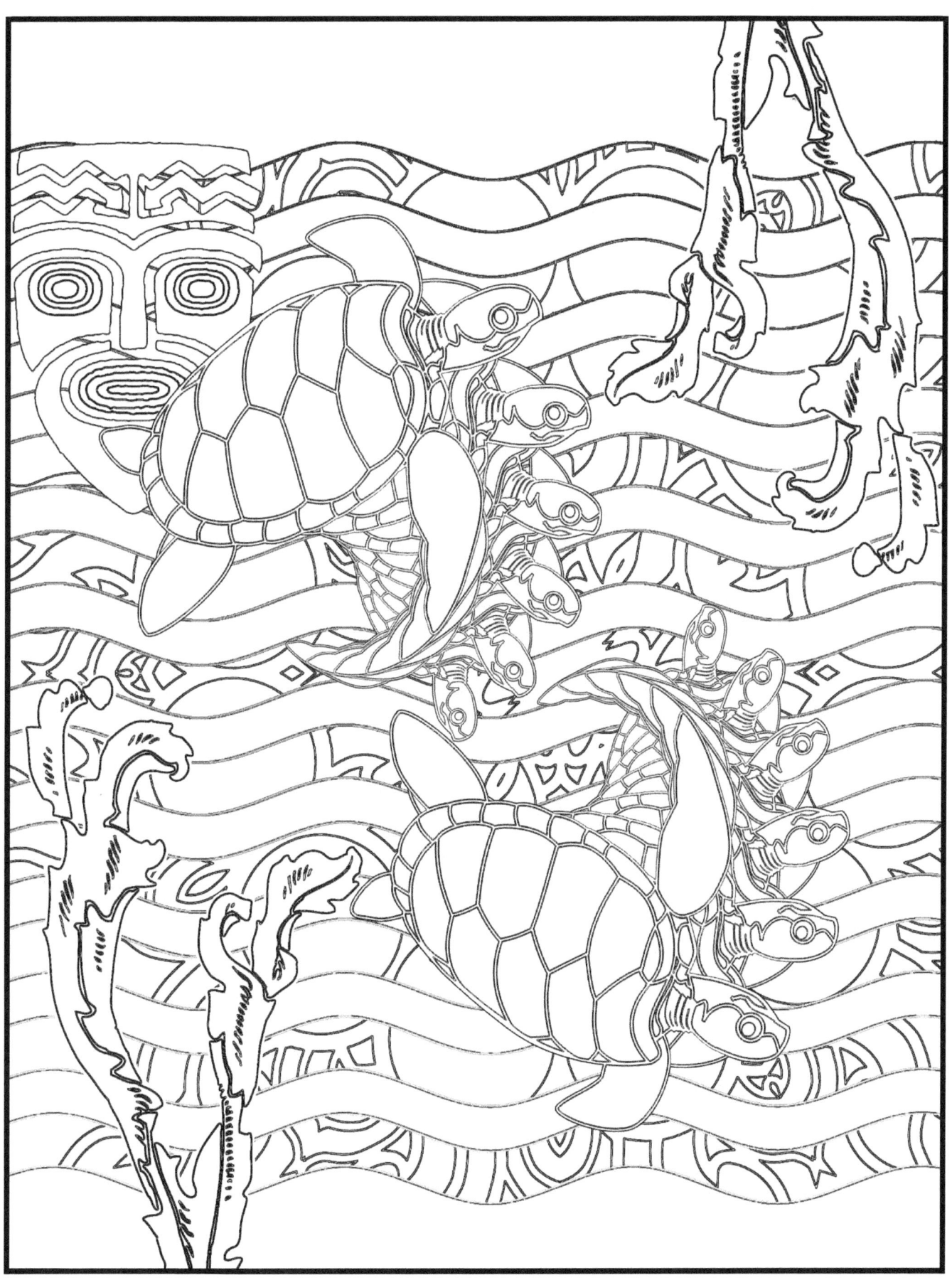

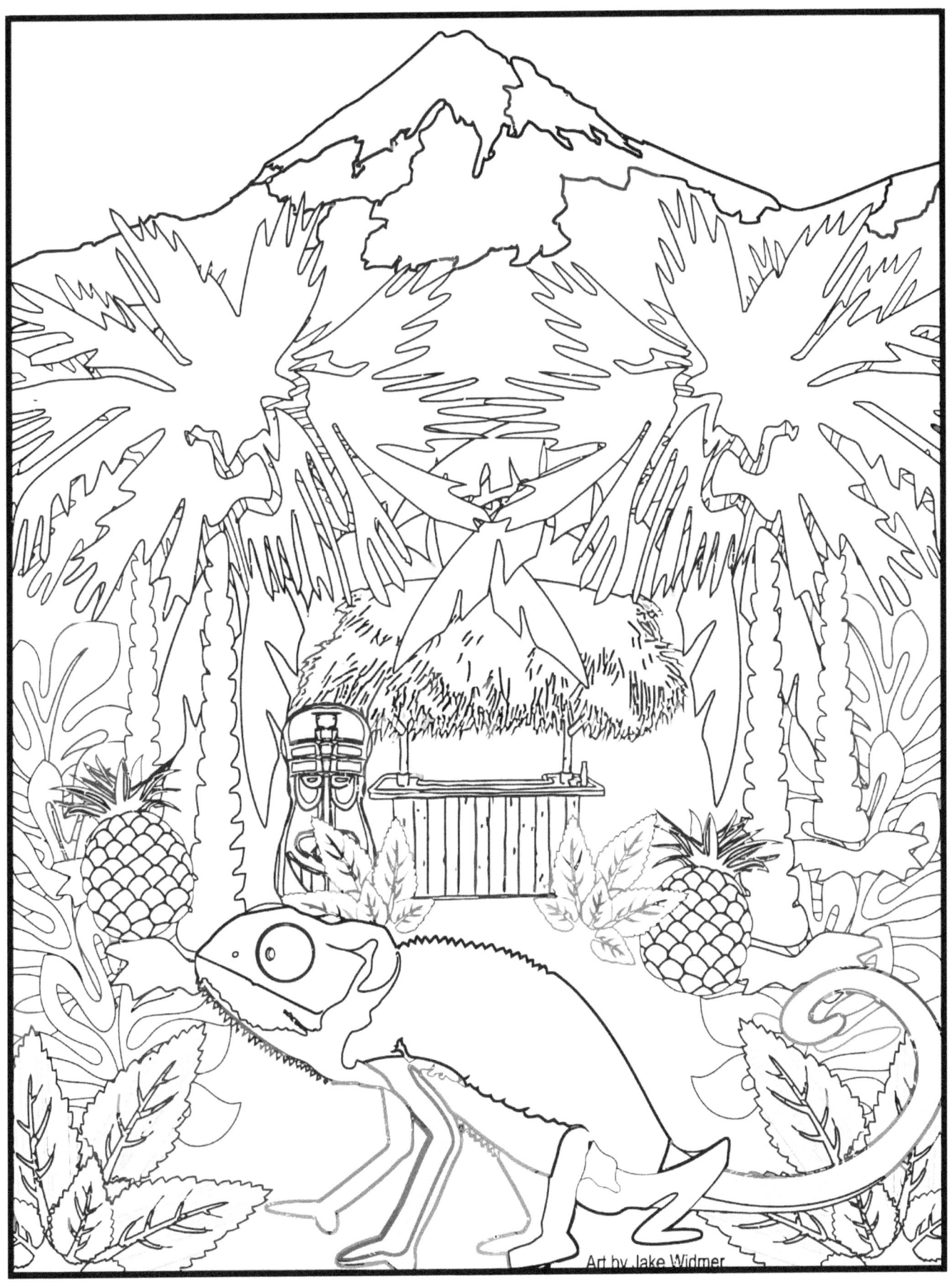

Art by Jake Widmer

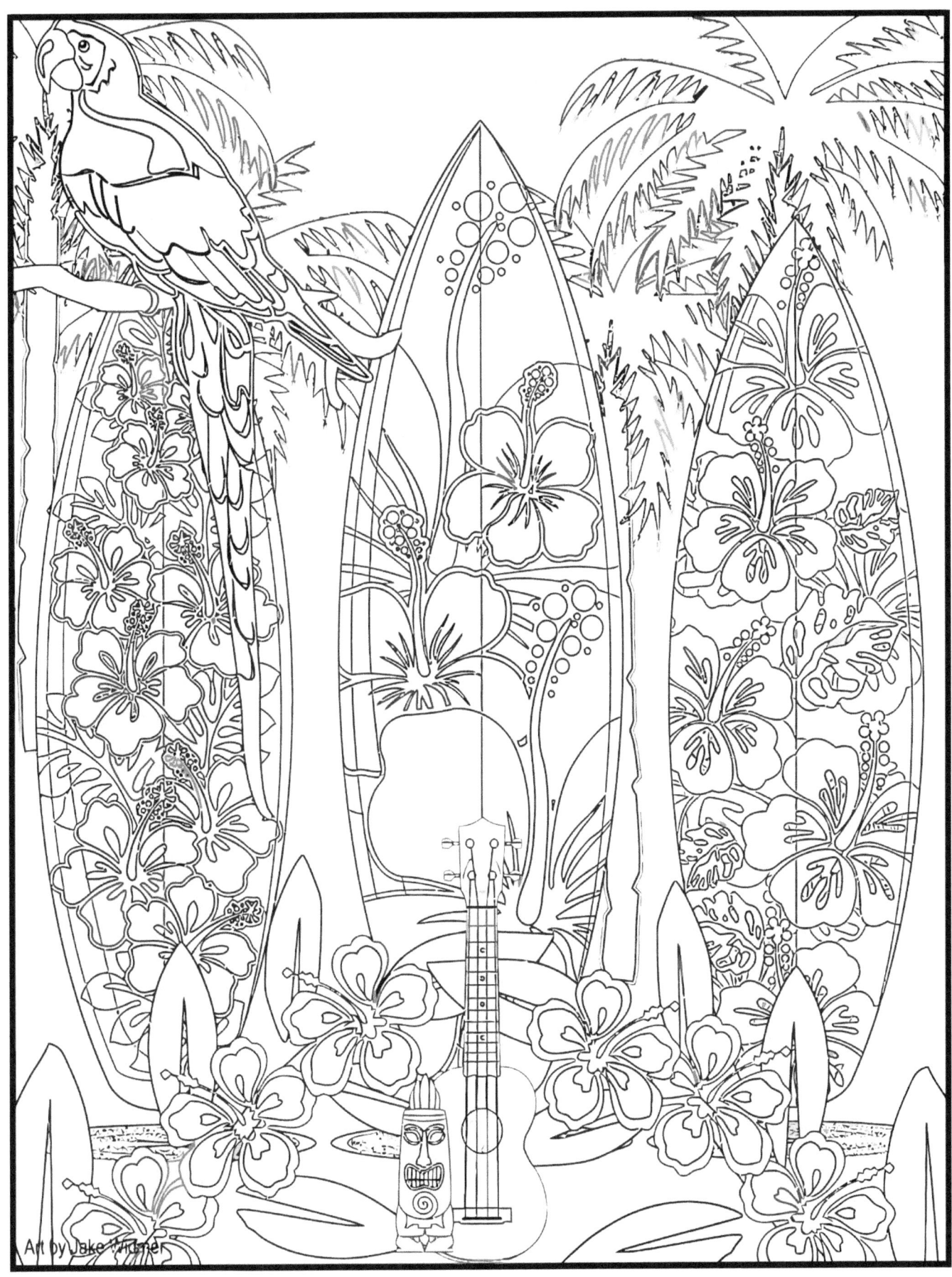

Art by Jake Widner

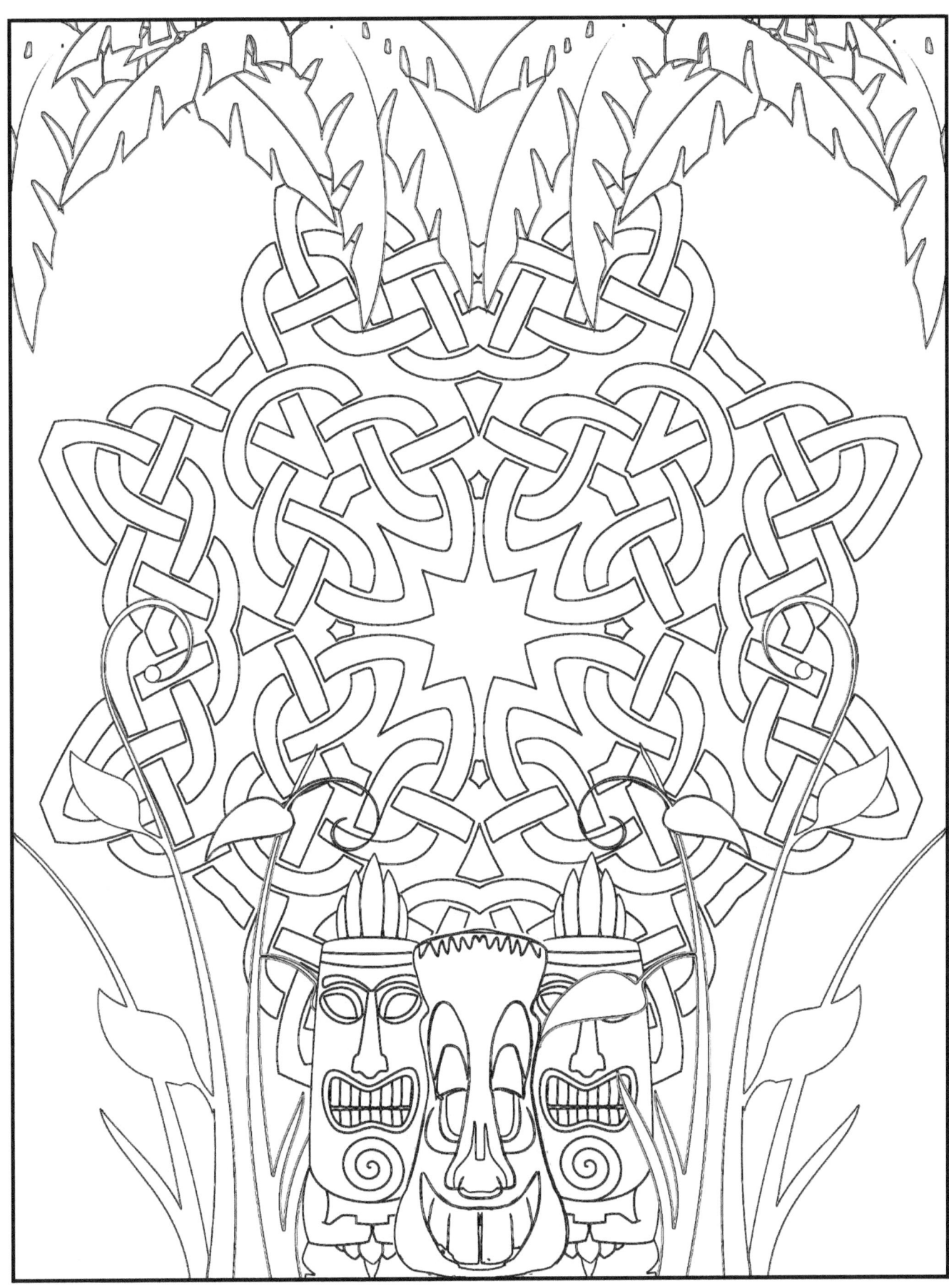

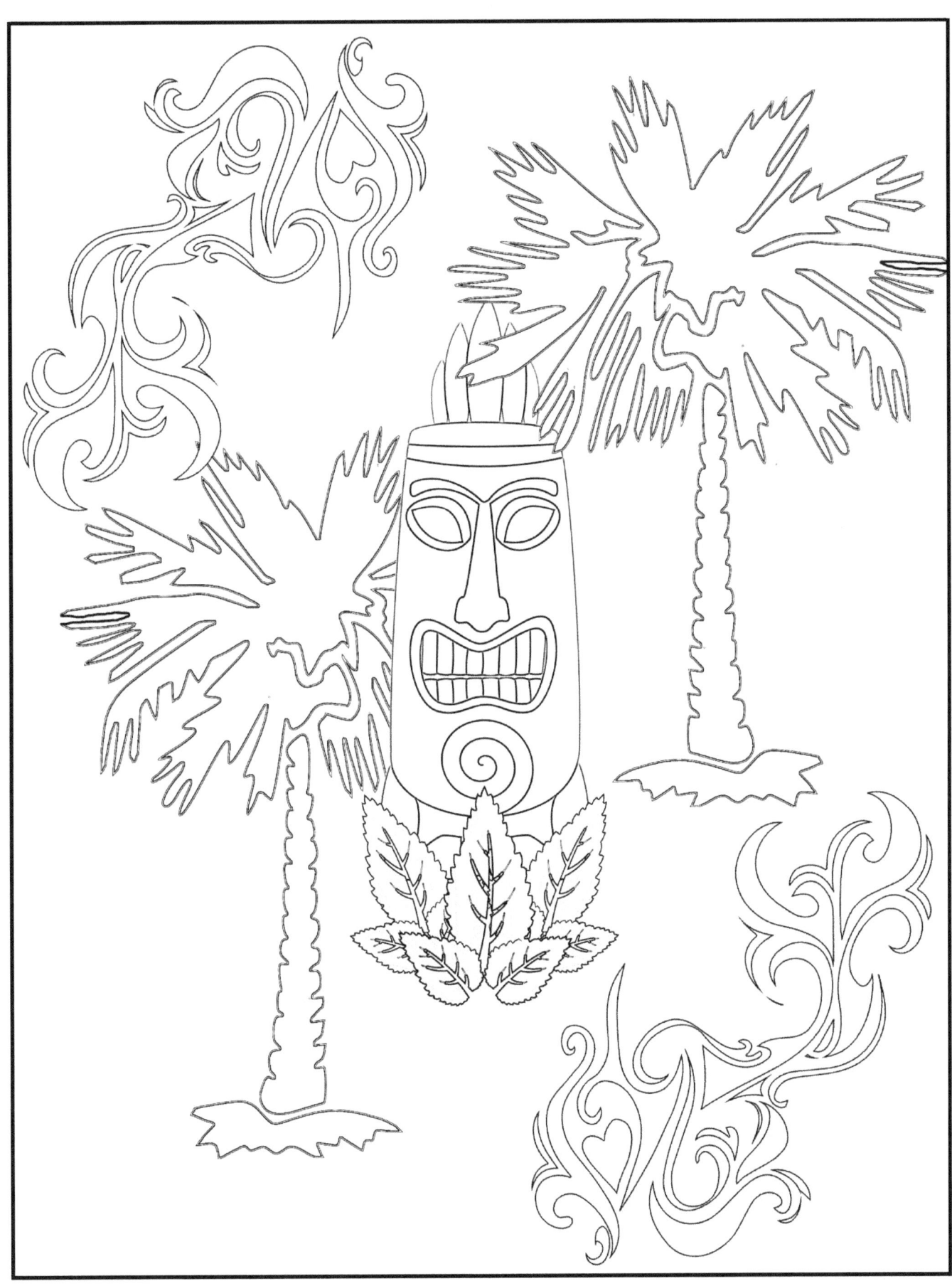

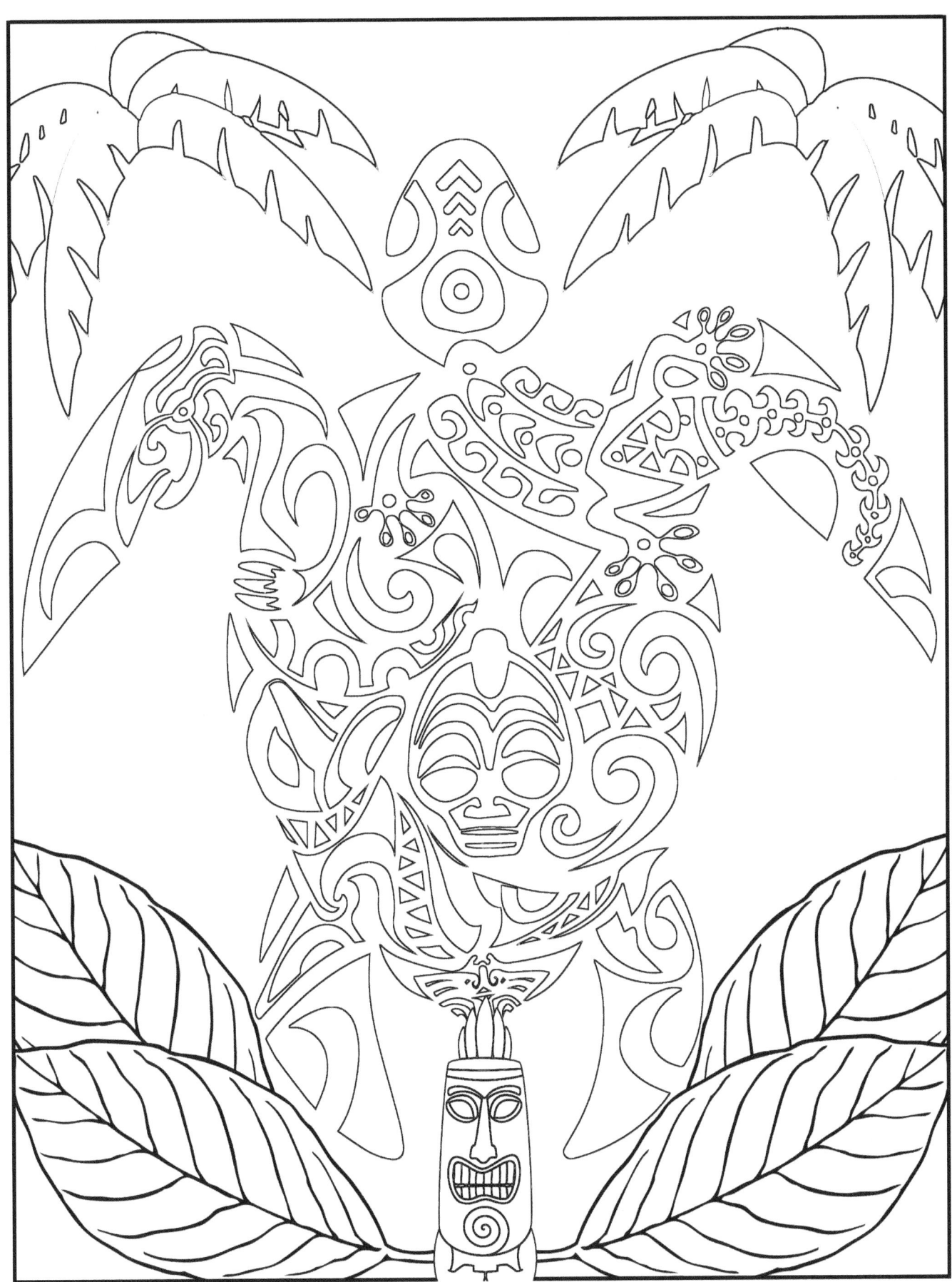

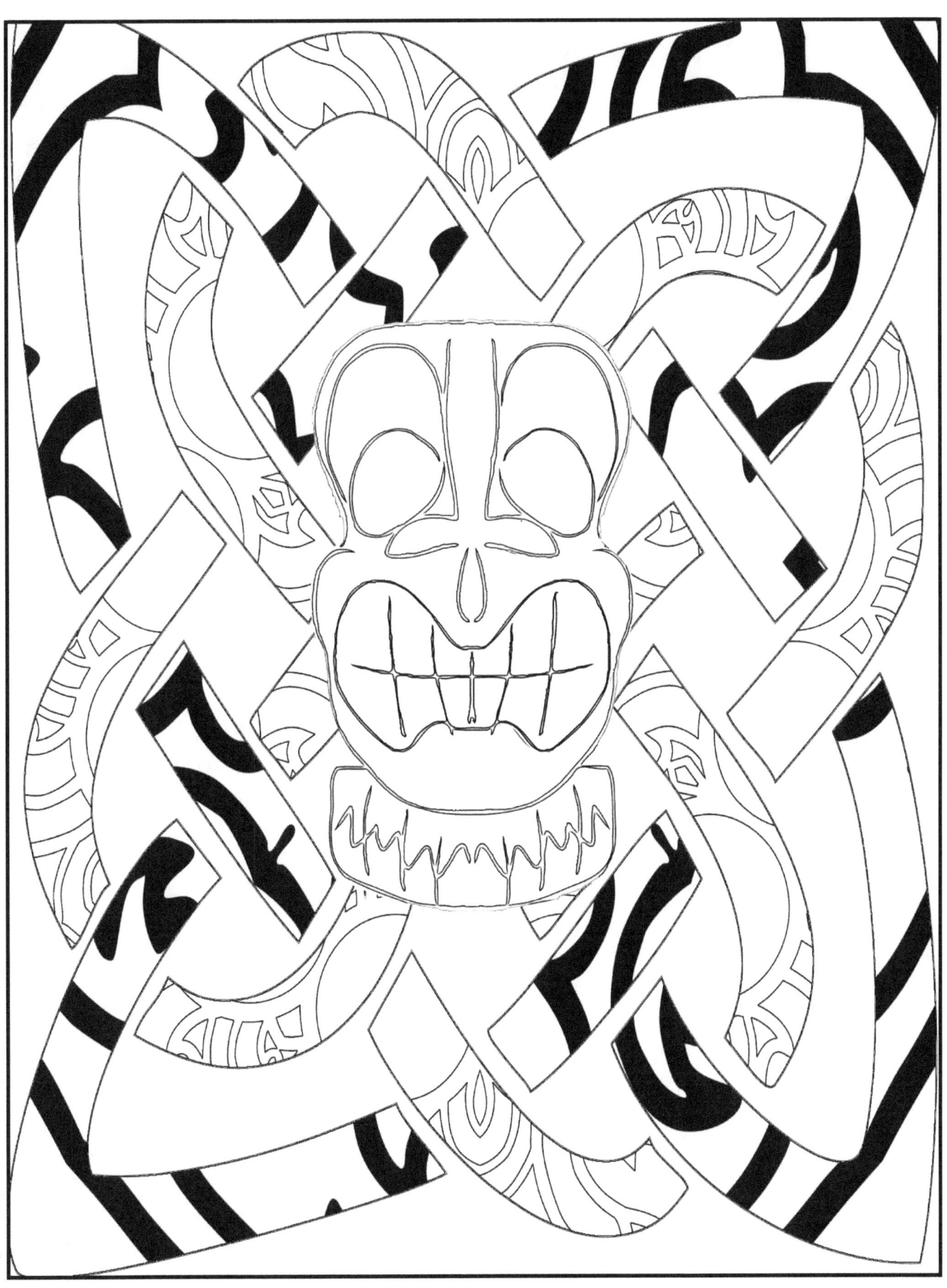

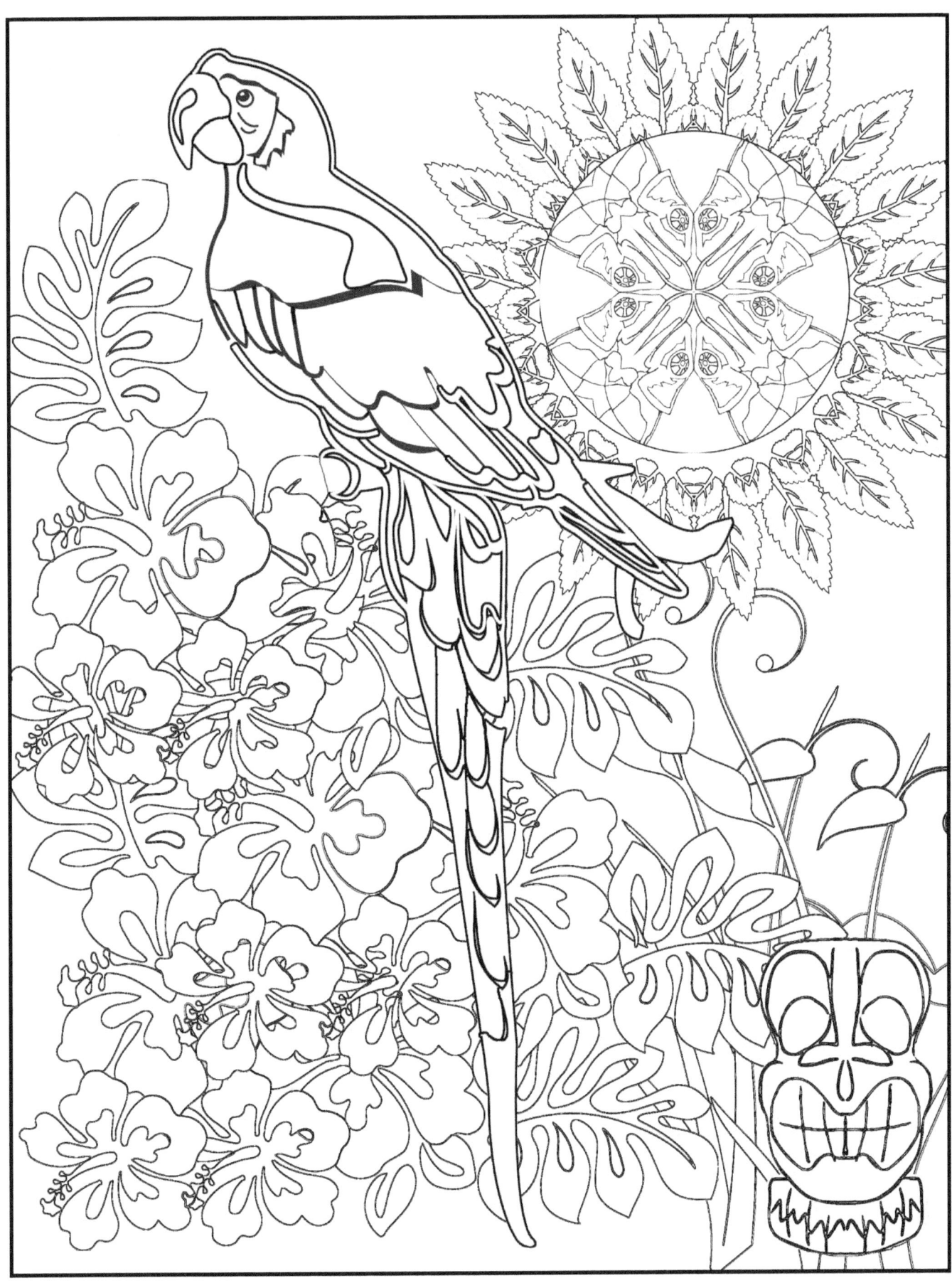

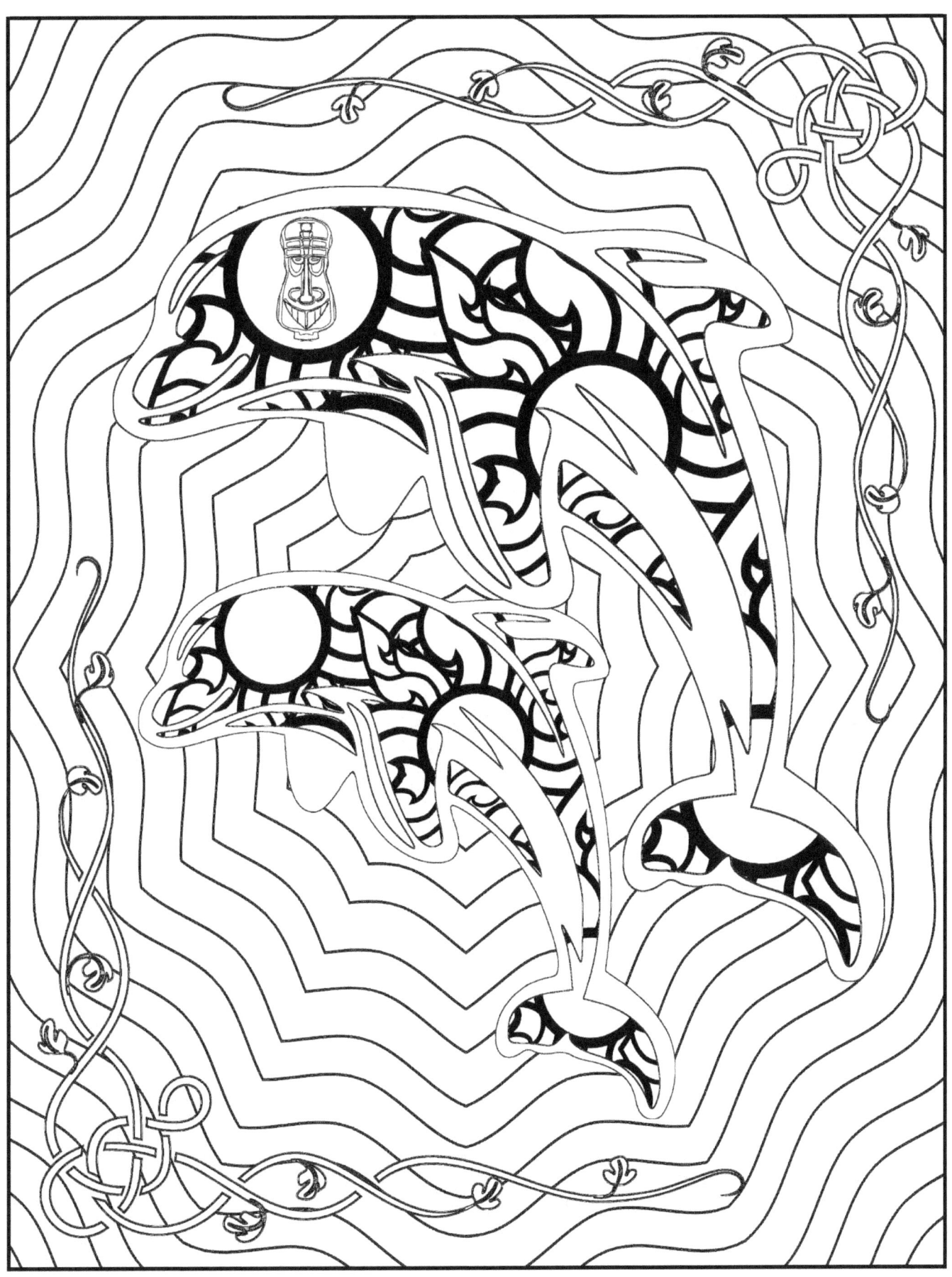

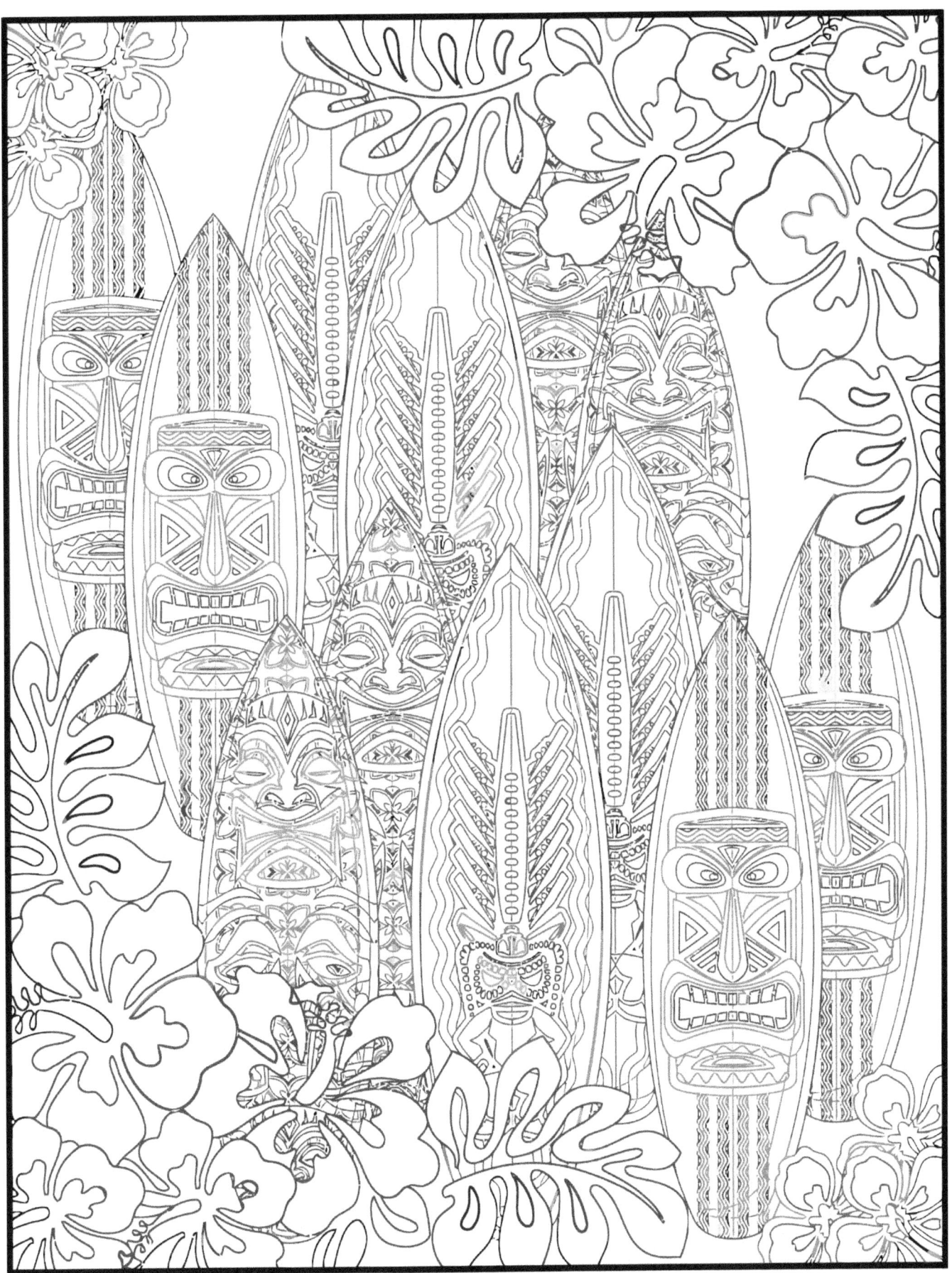

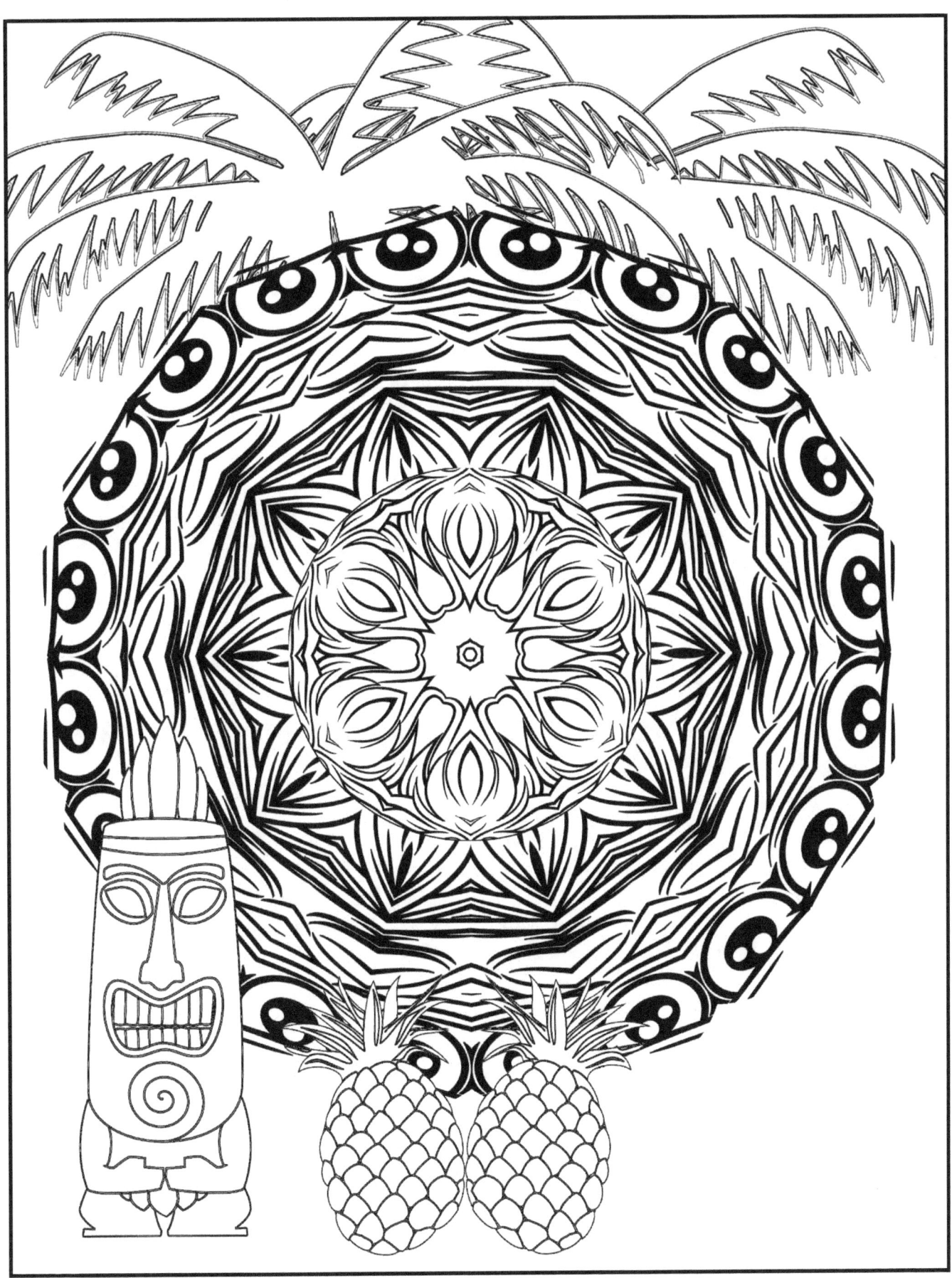

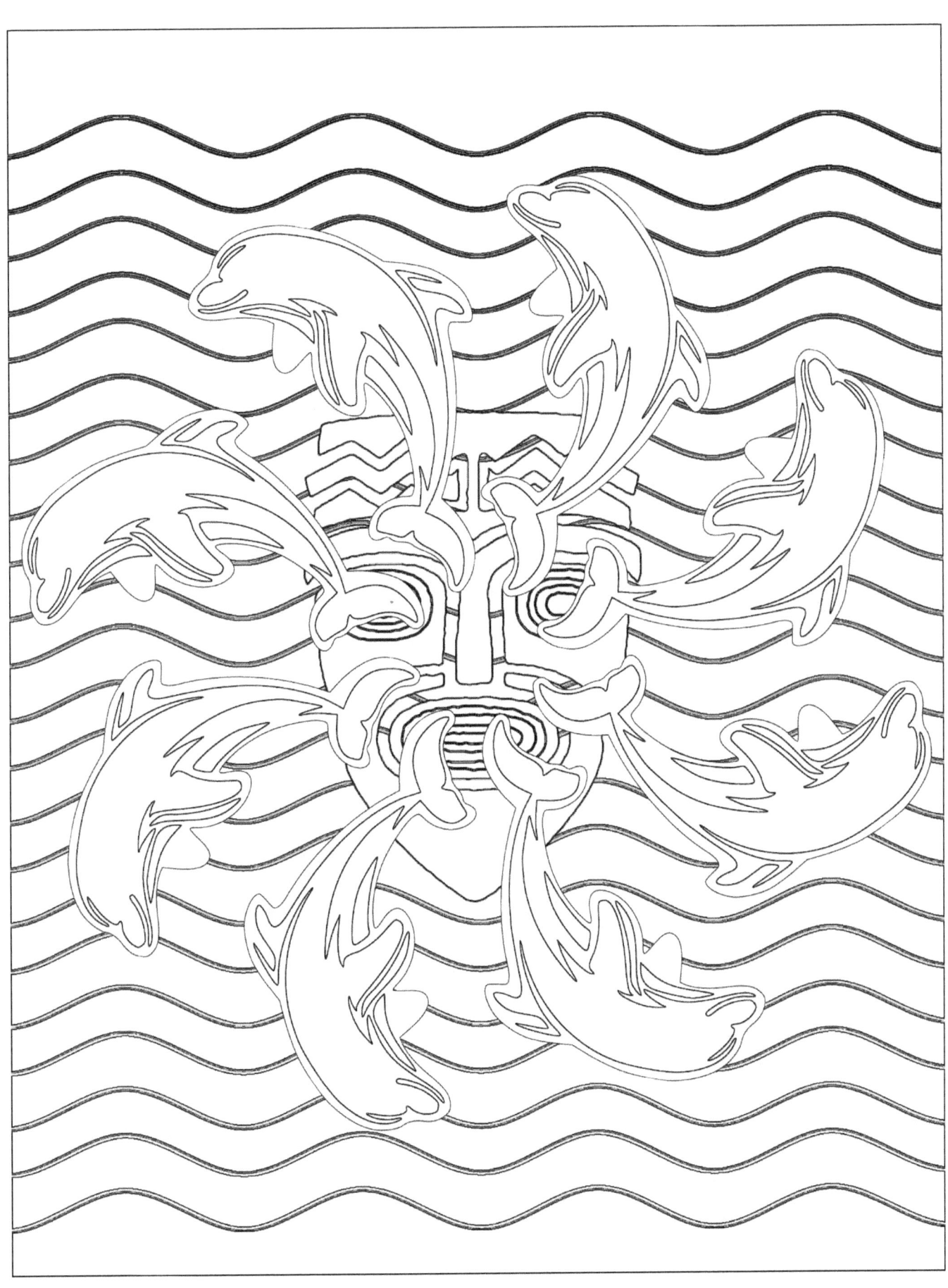

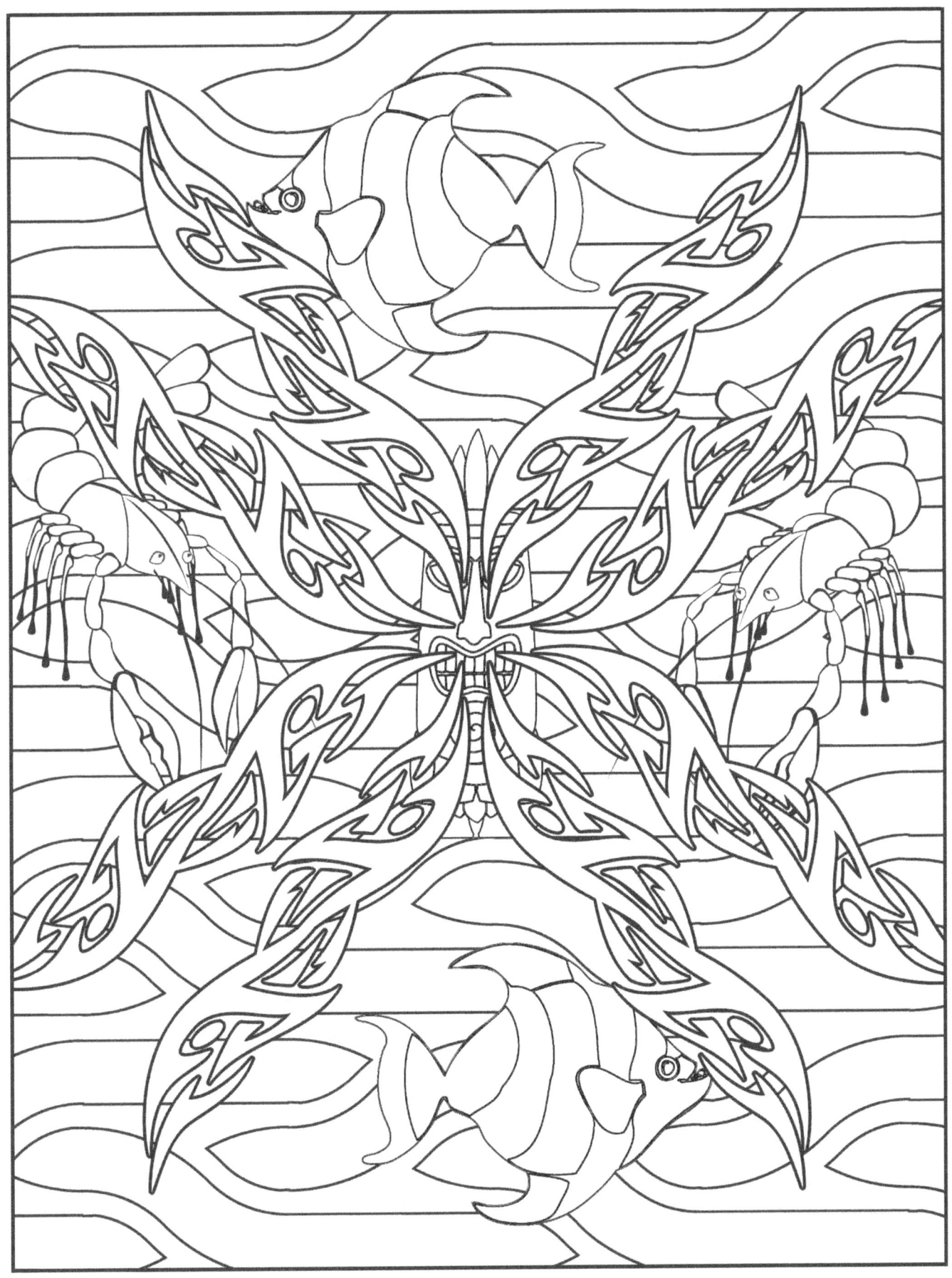

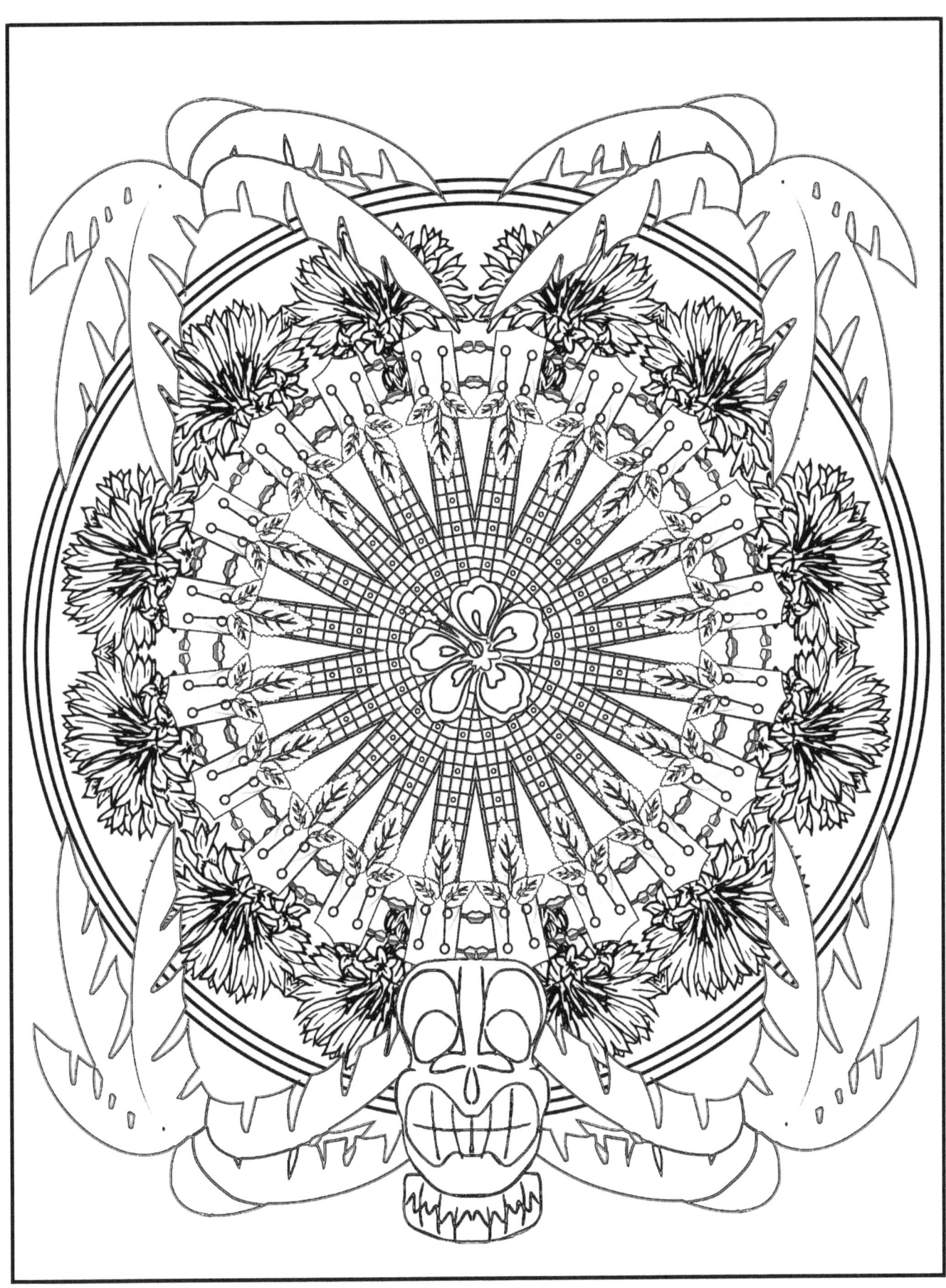

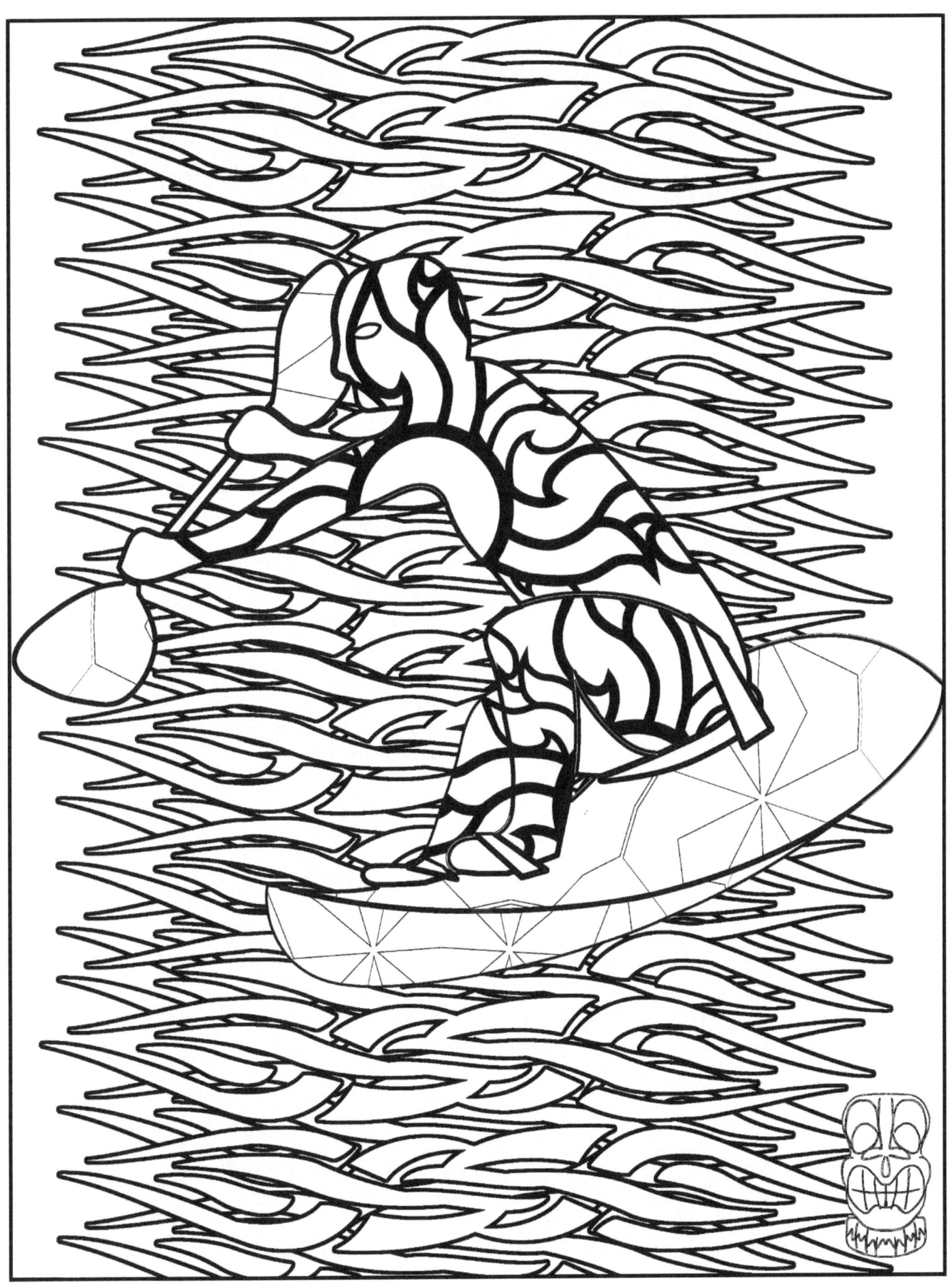

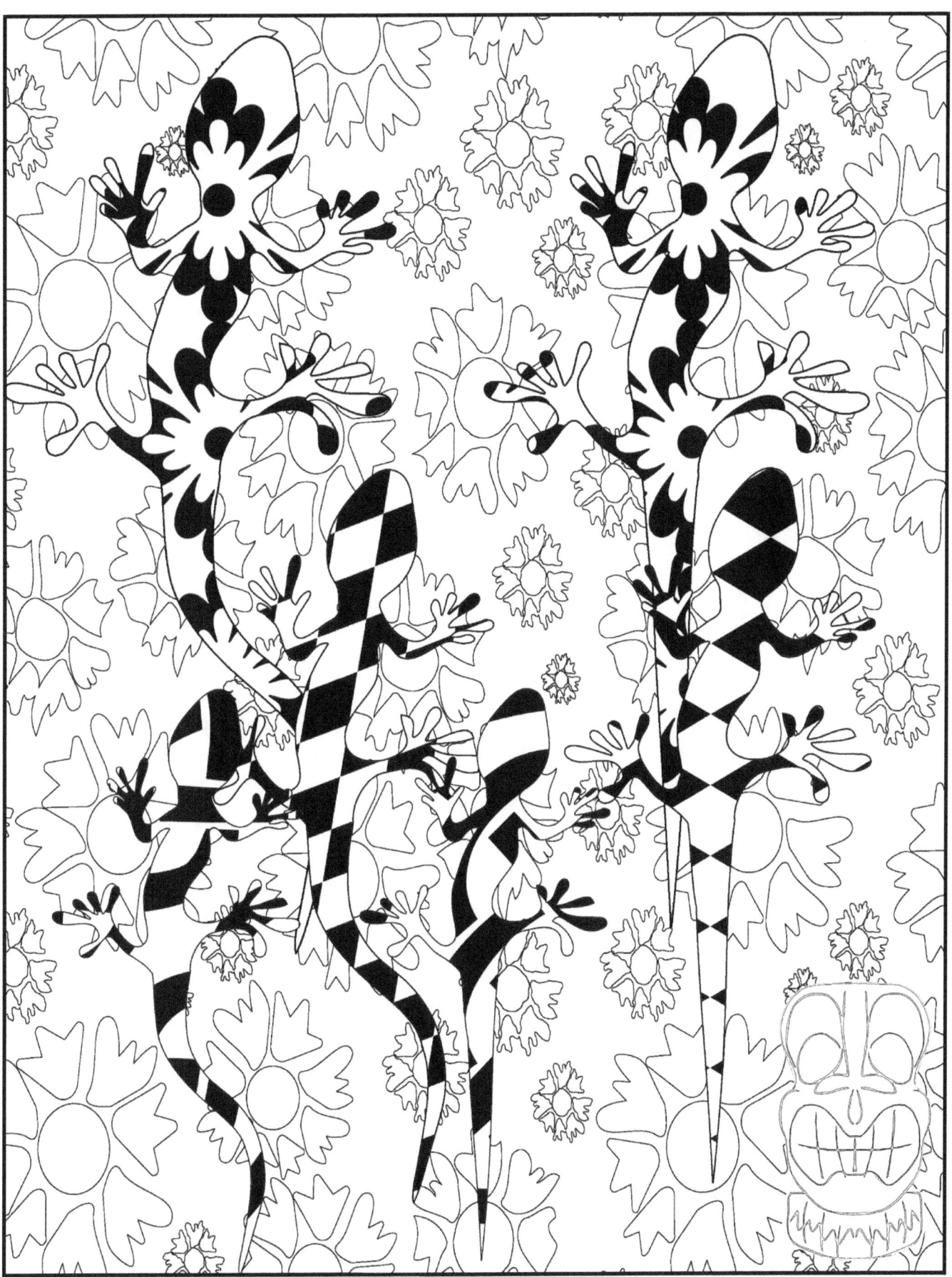

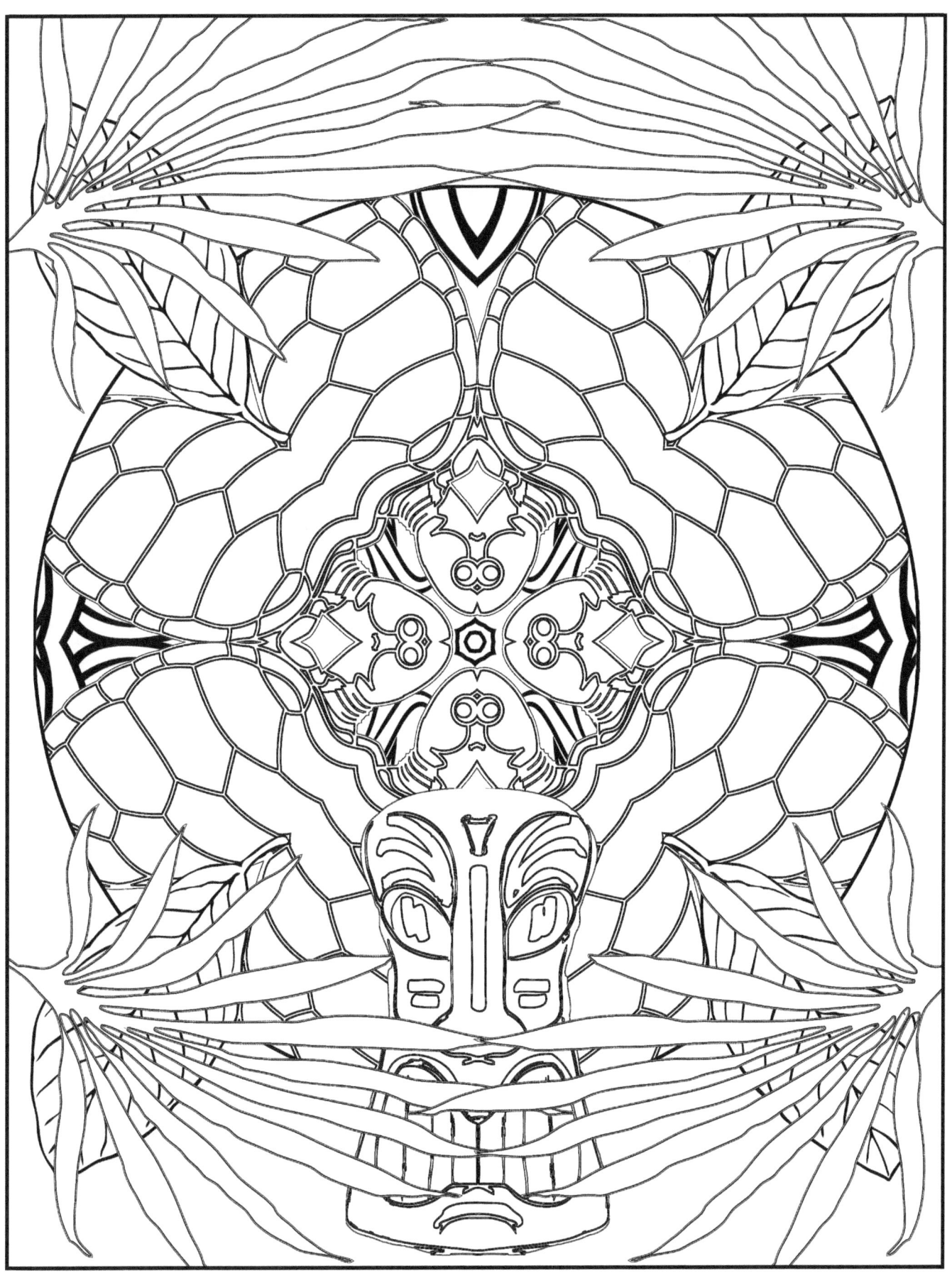

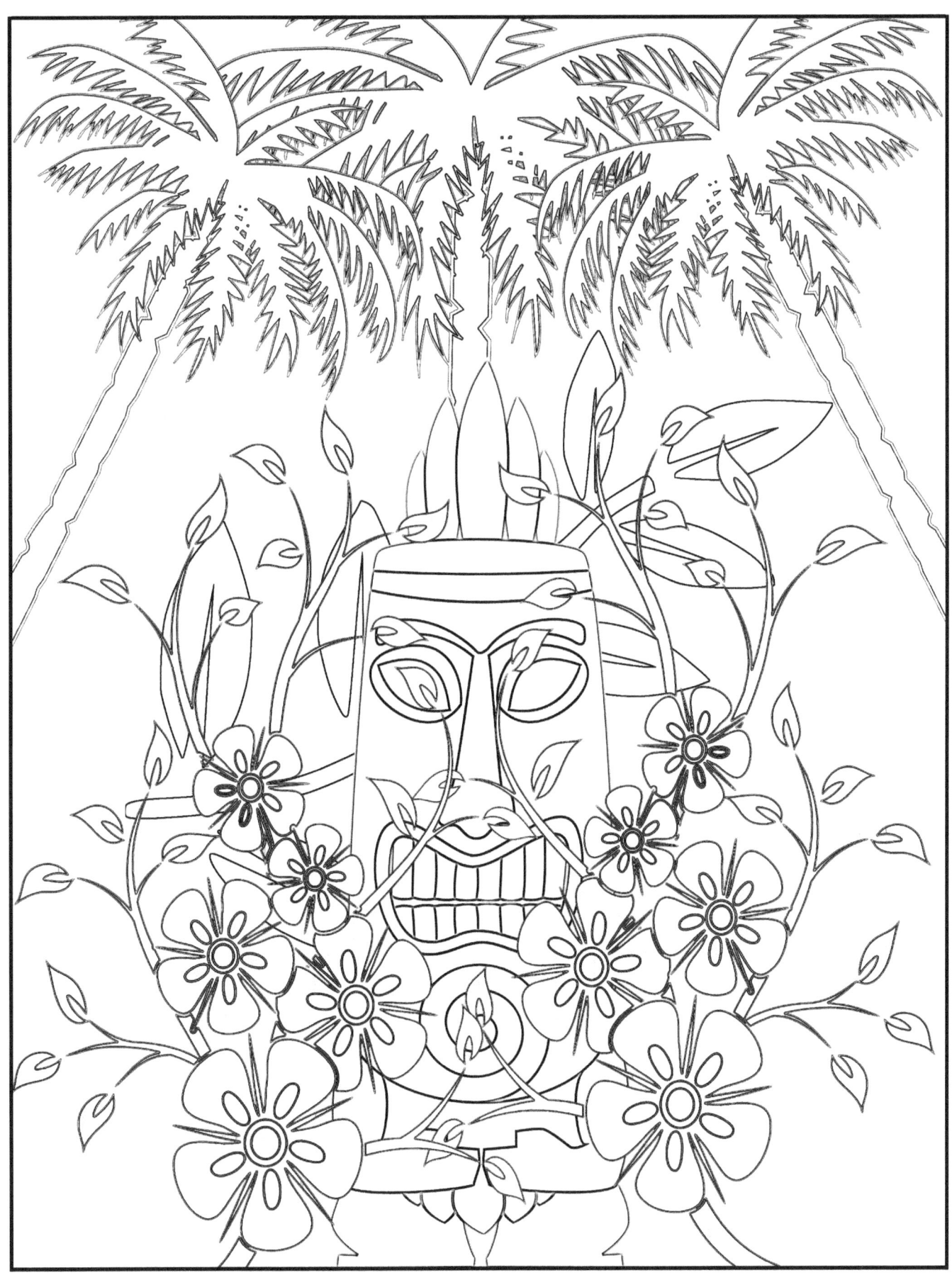

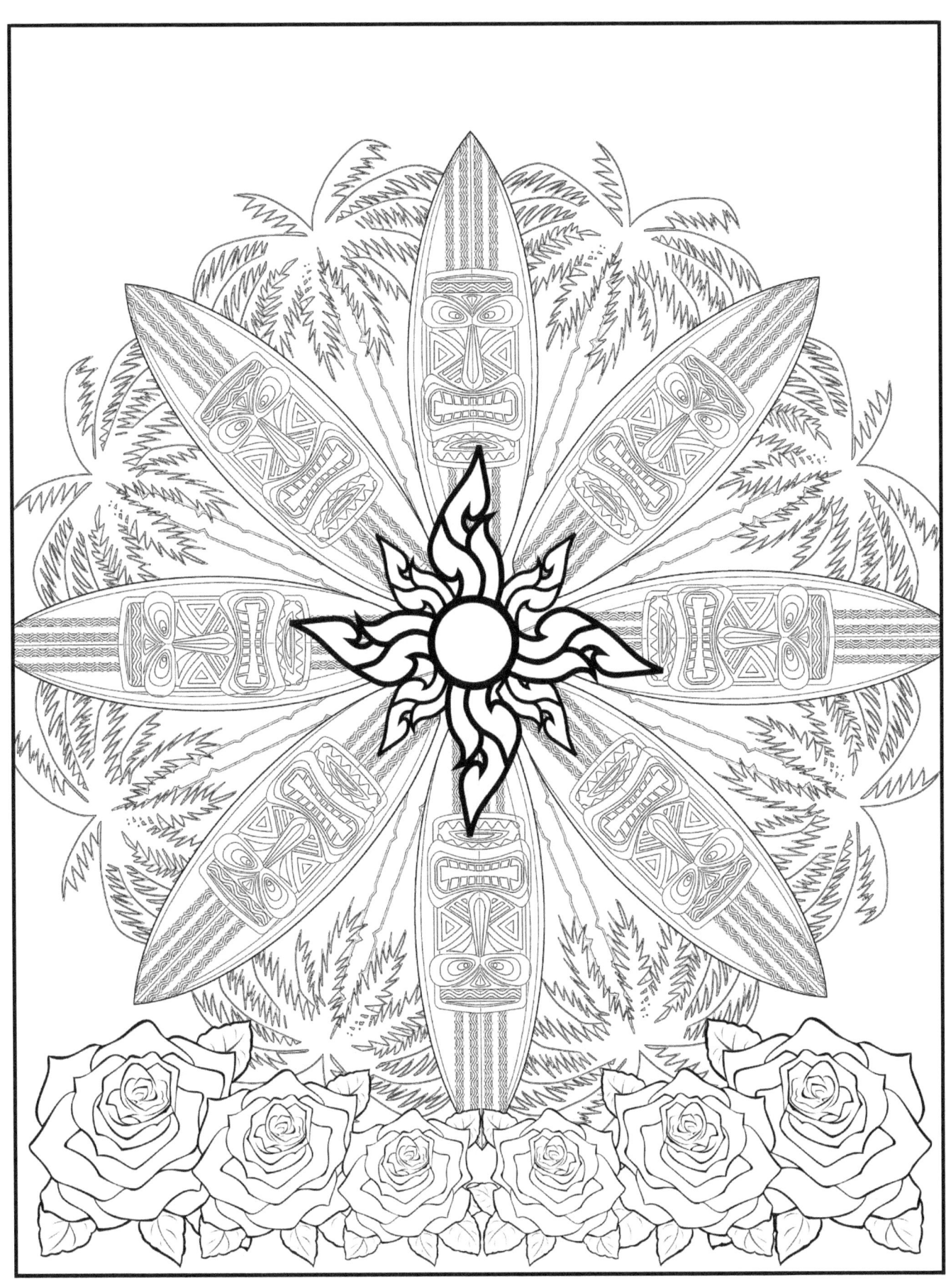

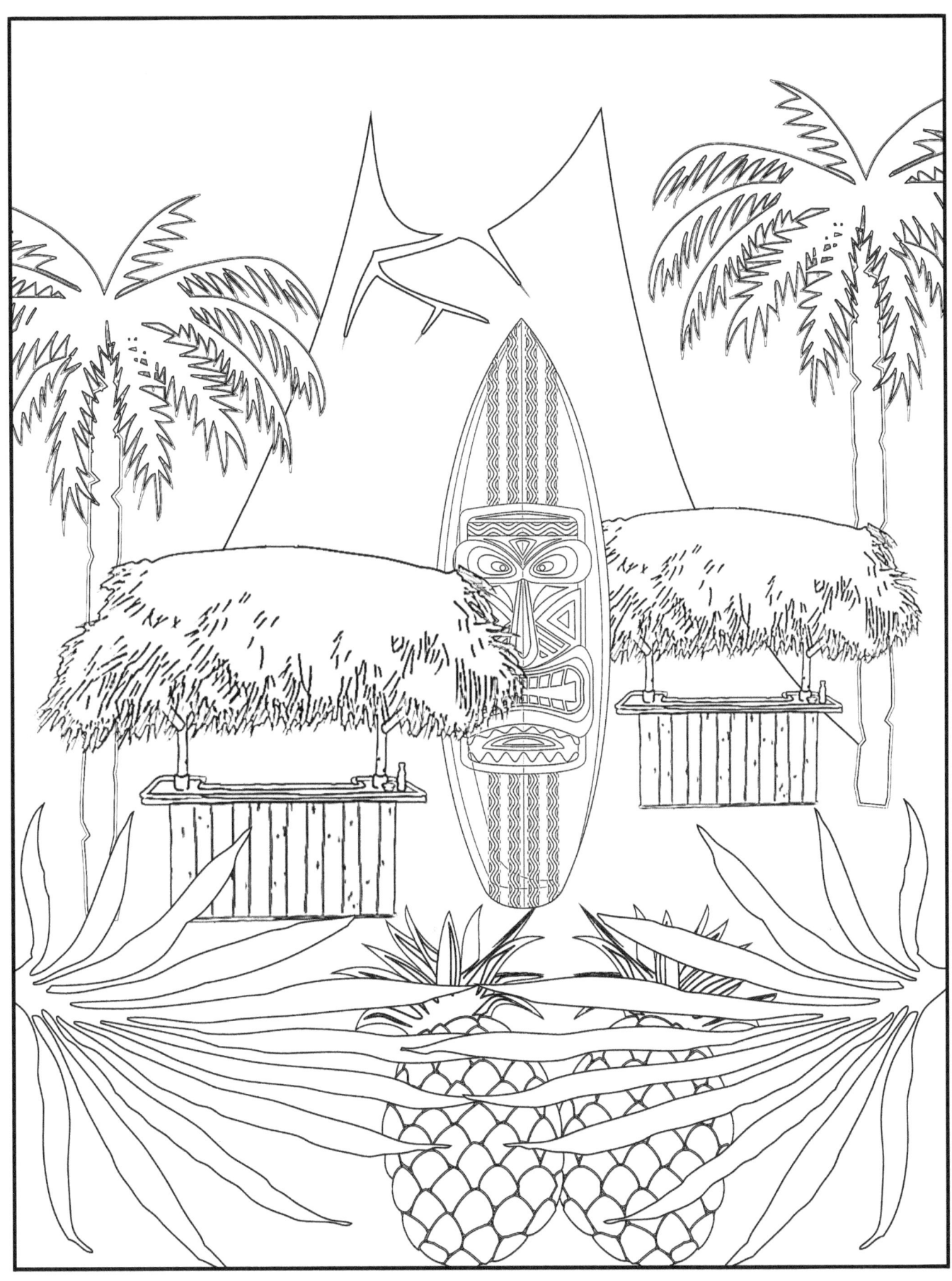

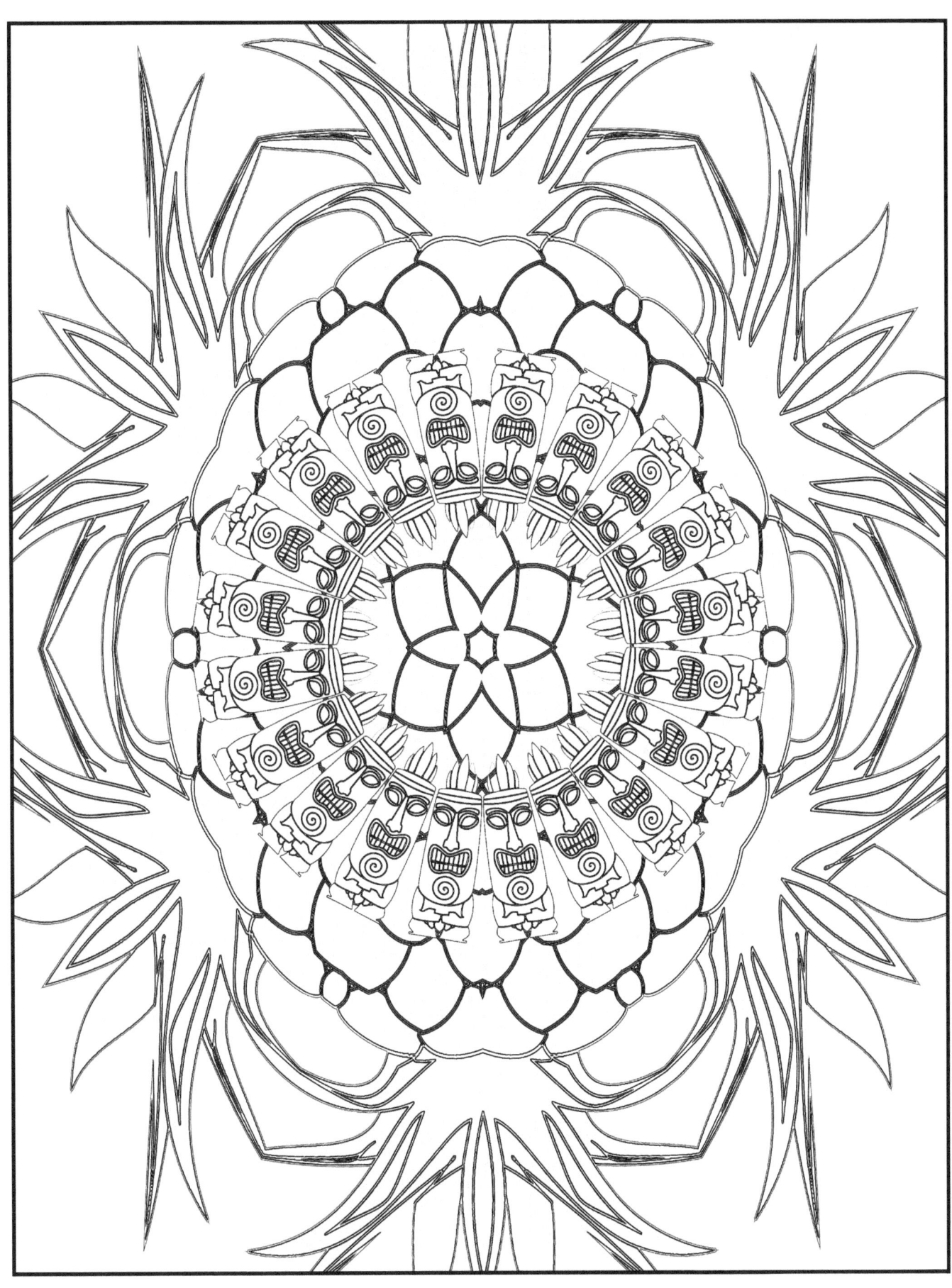

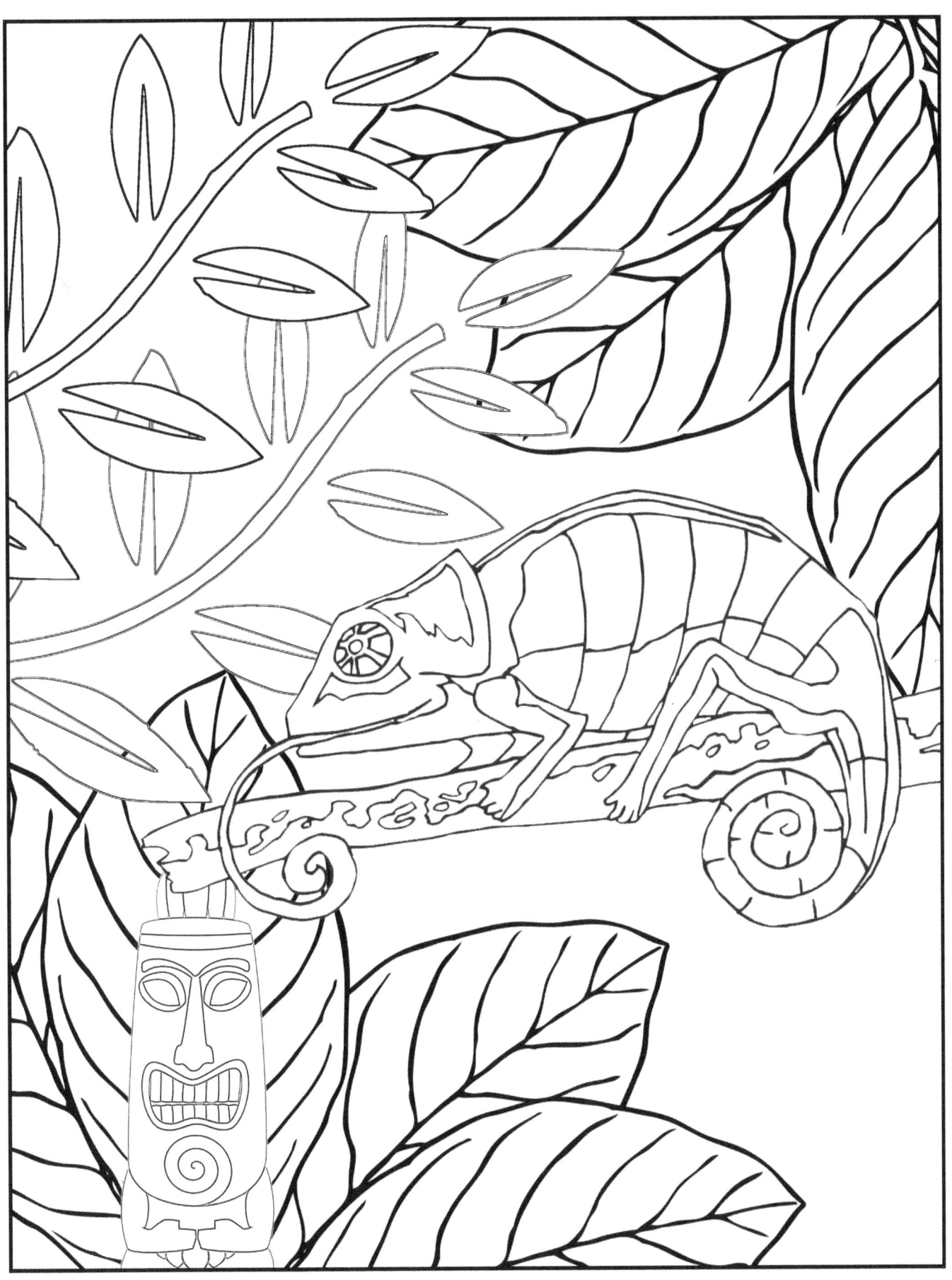

Clippee Coloring Books Wants to Thank You for Your Purchase

To Show Our Gratitude
We Would Like to Give You a Free Coloring Book Page Every Week

Just Go to Clippee **Coloring** and Subscribe to Join Our Private Facebook Group and You Can Download Past and Future Pages!!

Have an Amazing Day from Clippee! And Dont Forget to Confirm Your Email Address☺

<u>Clippee.com</u>

Other Books by Clippee Coloring

Mexican Vacation – Clippee.com/mexico

www.ingramcontent.com/pod-product-compliance
Lightning Source LLC
Chambersburg PA
CBHW080612180526
45168CB00007B/2885